Frogs Adult Coloring Book

This Coloring book belongs to:

_____

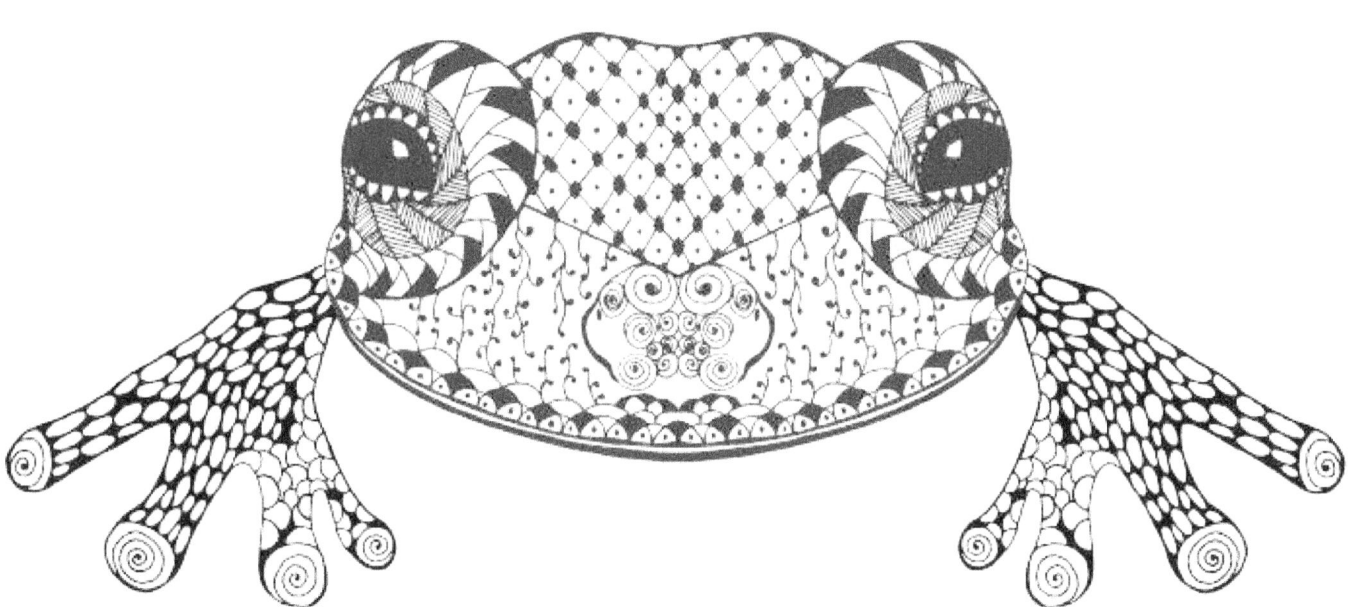

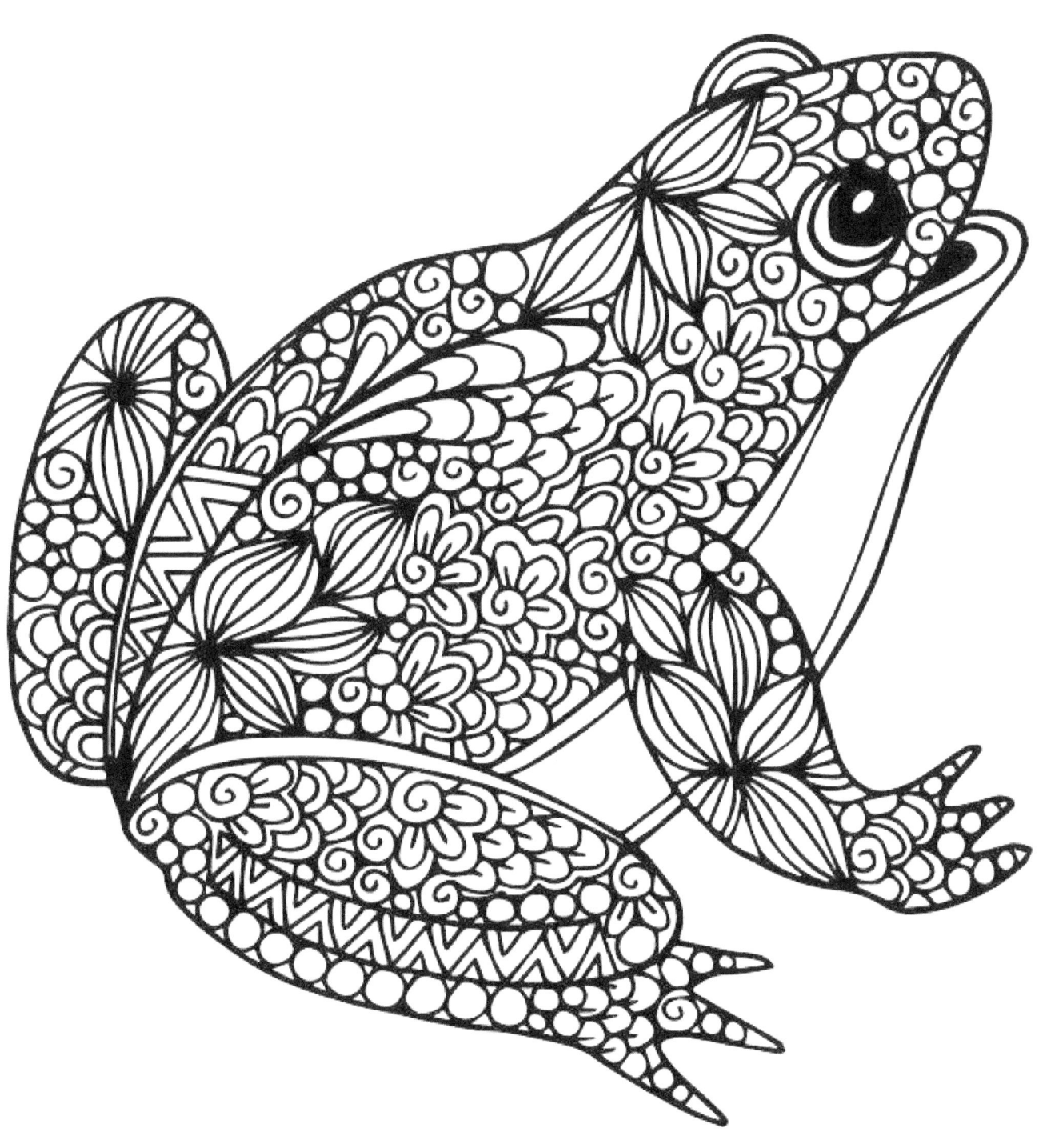

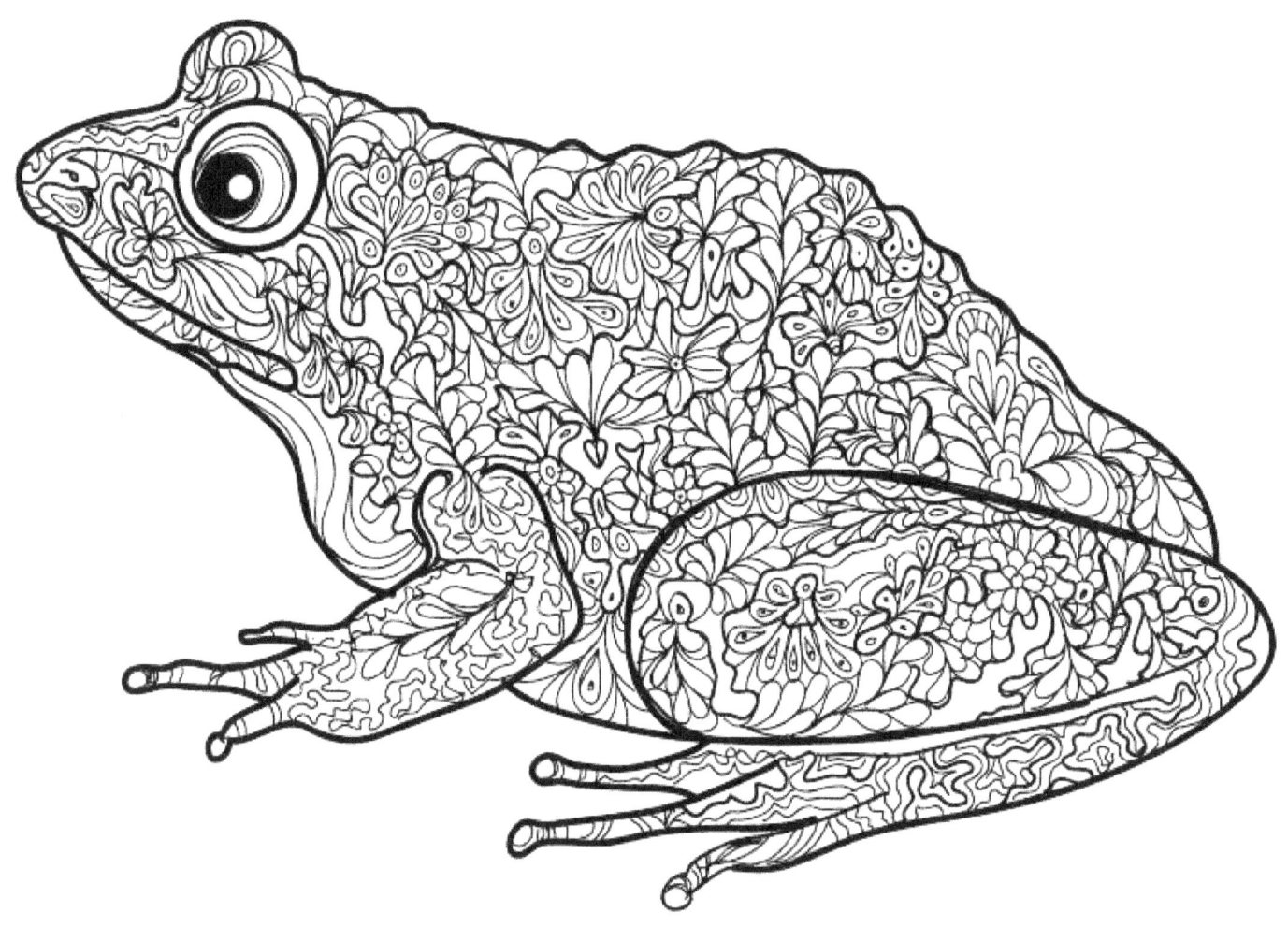

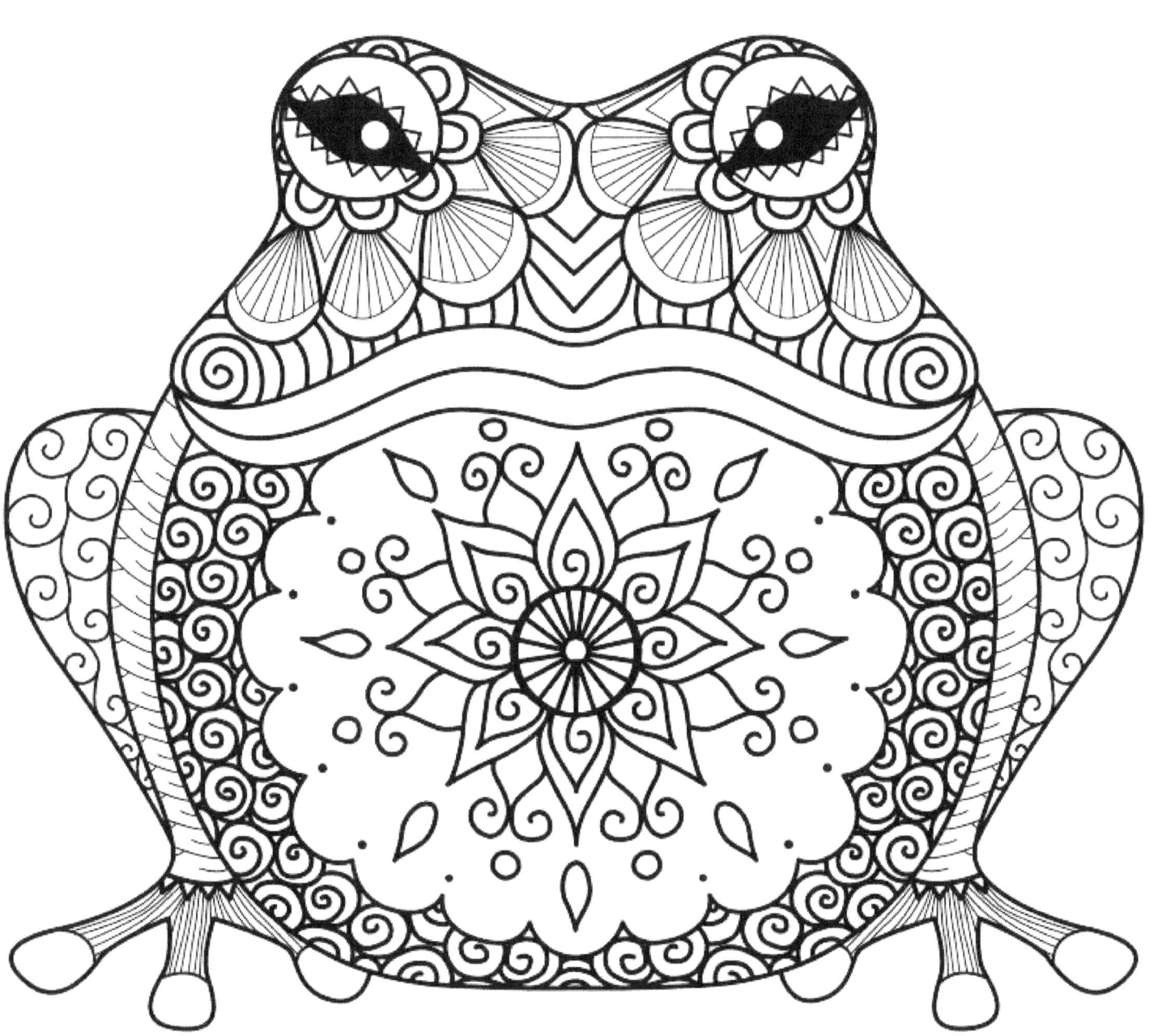

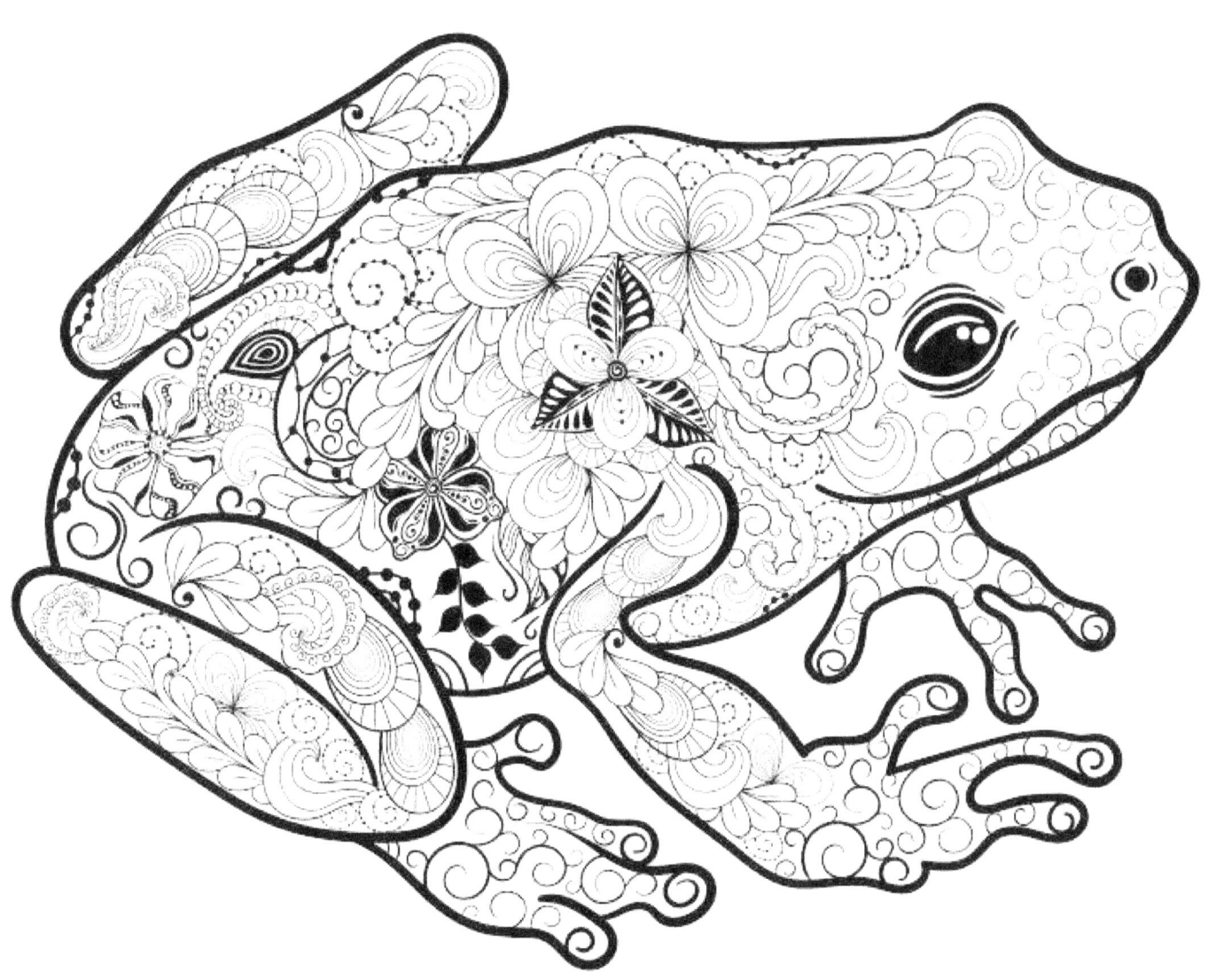

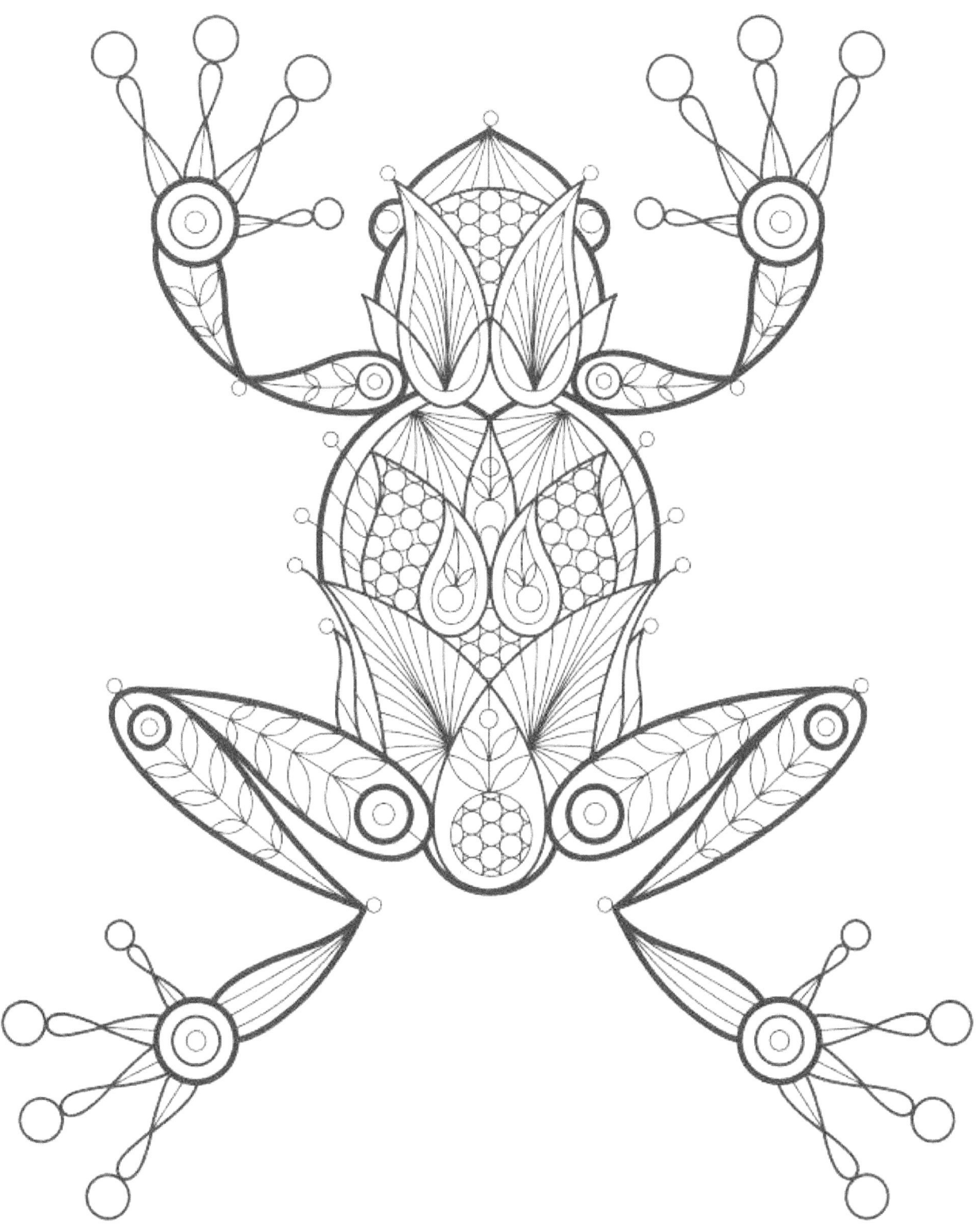

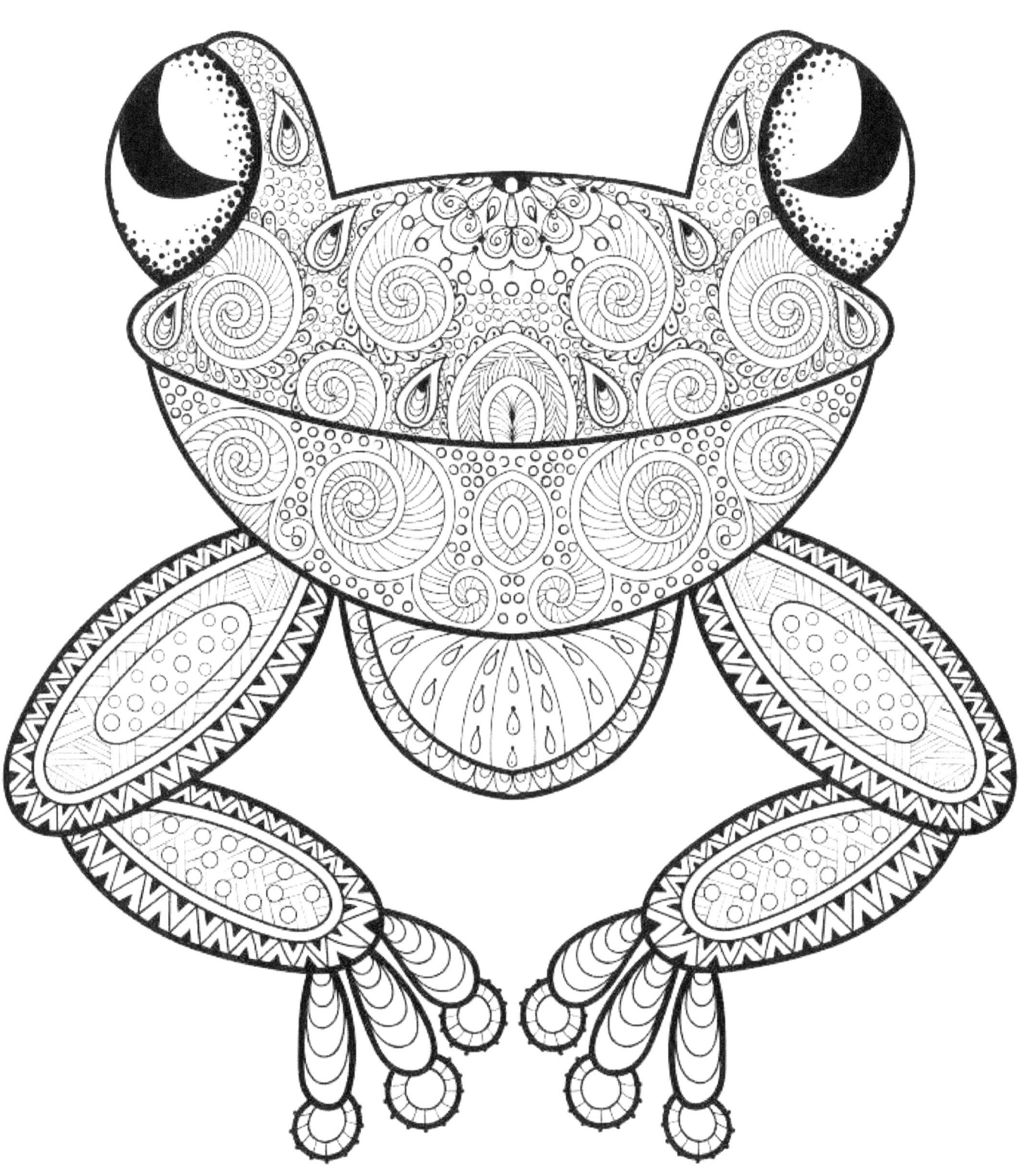

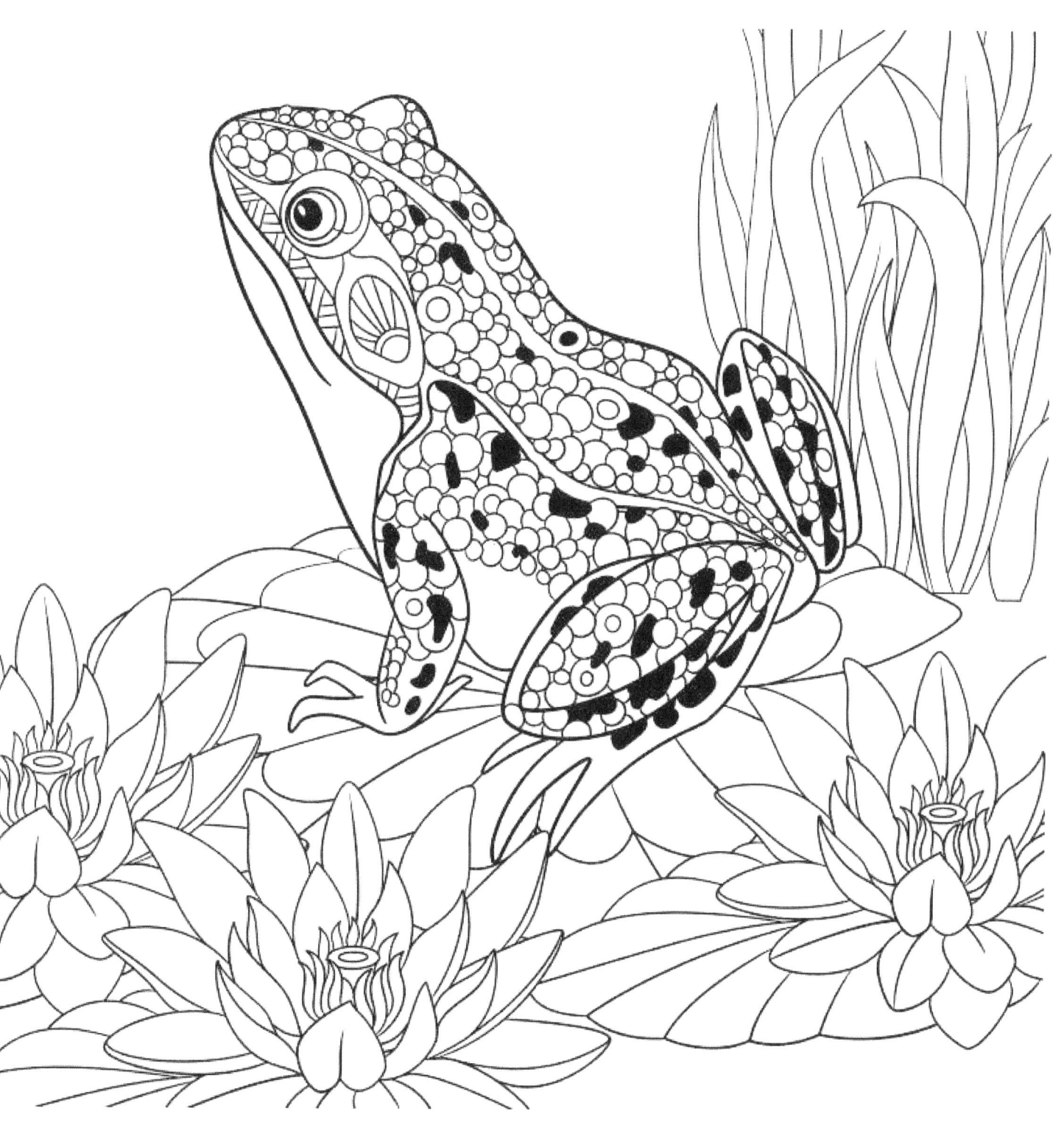

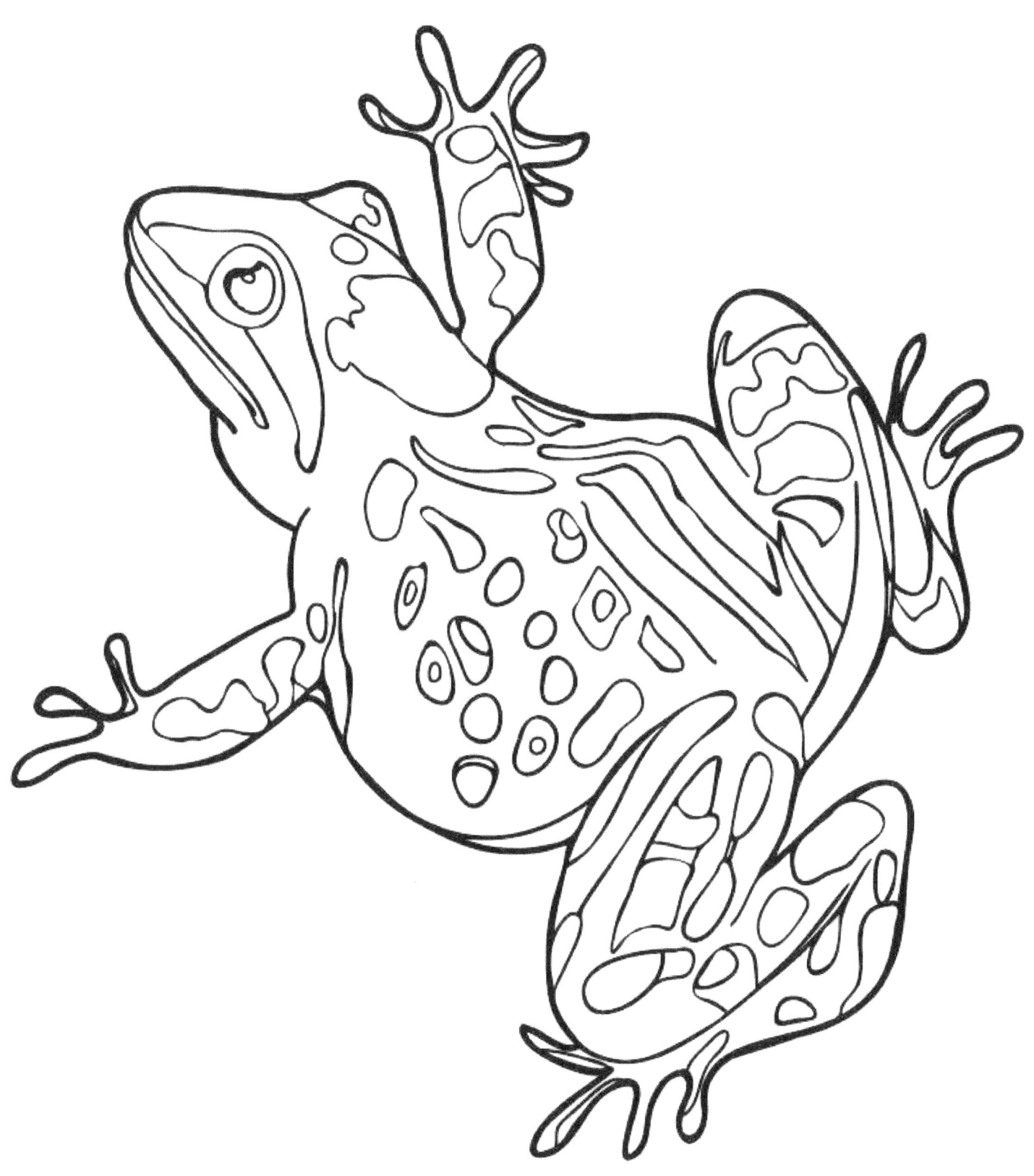

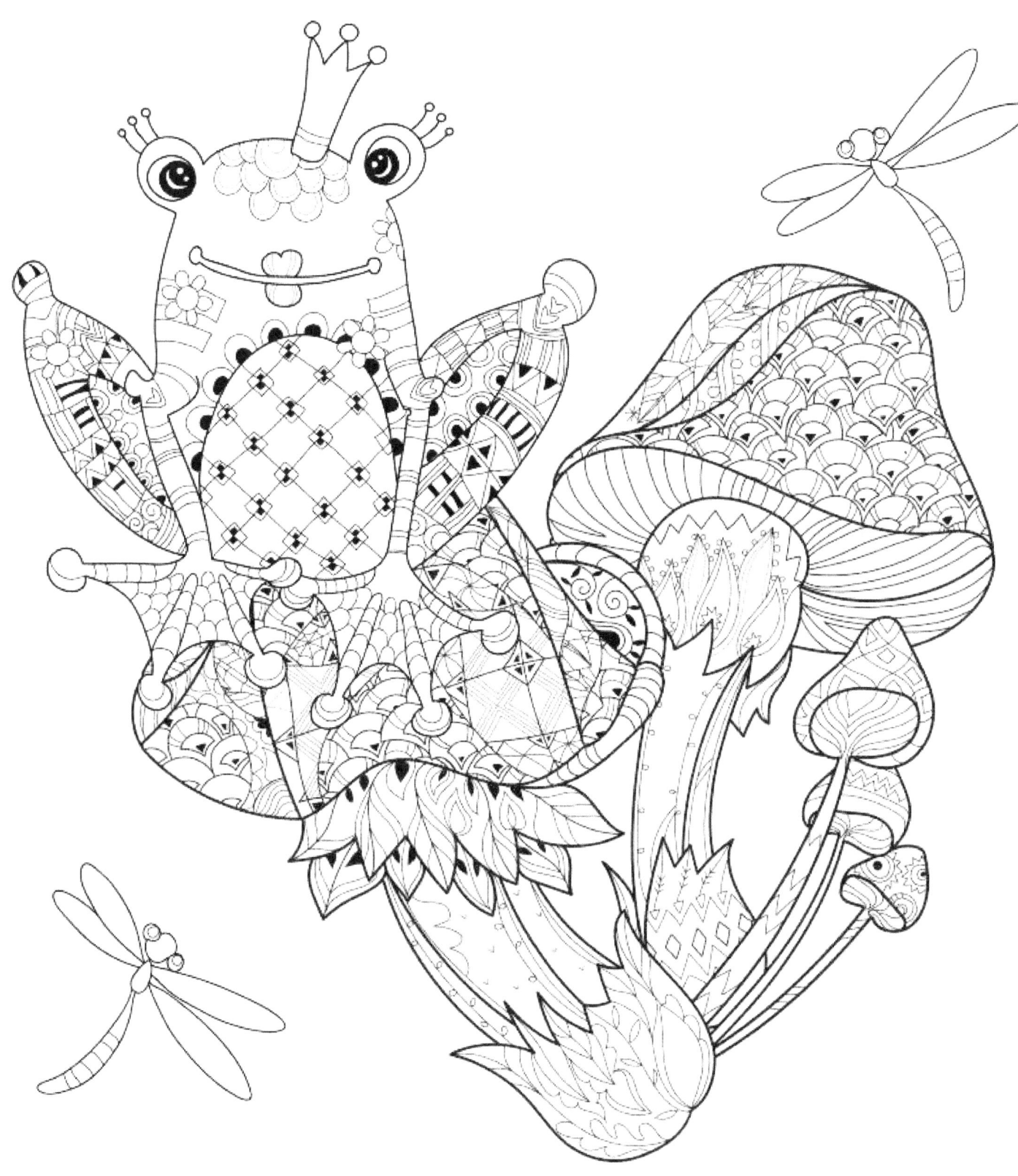

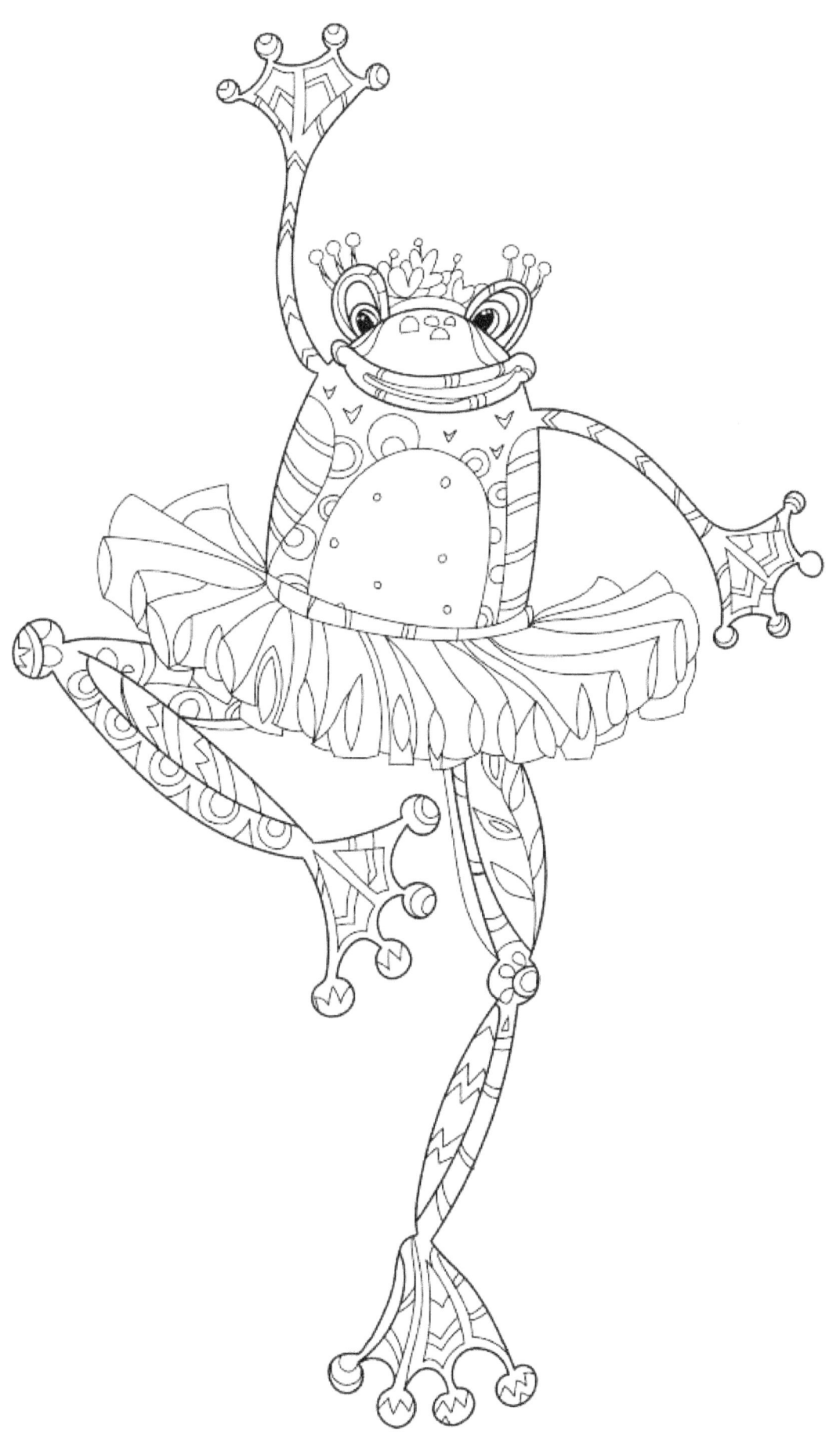

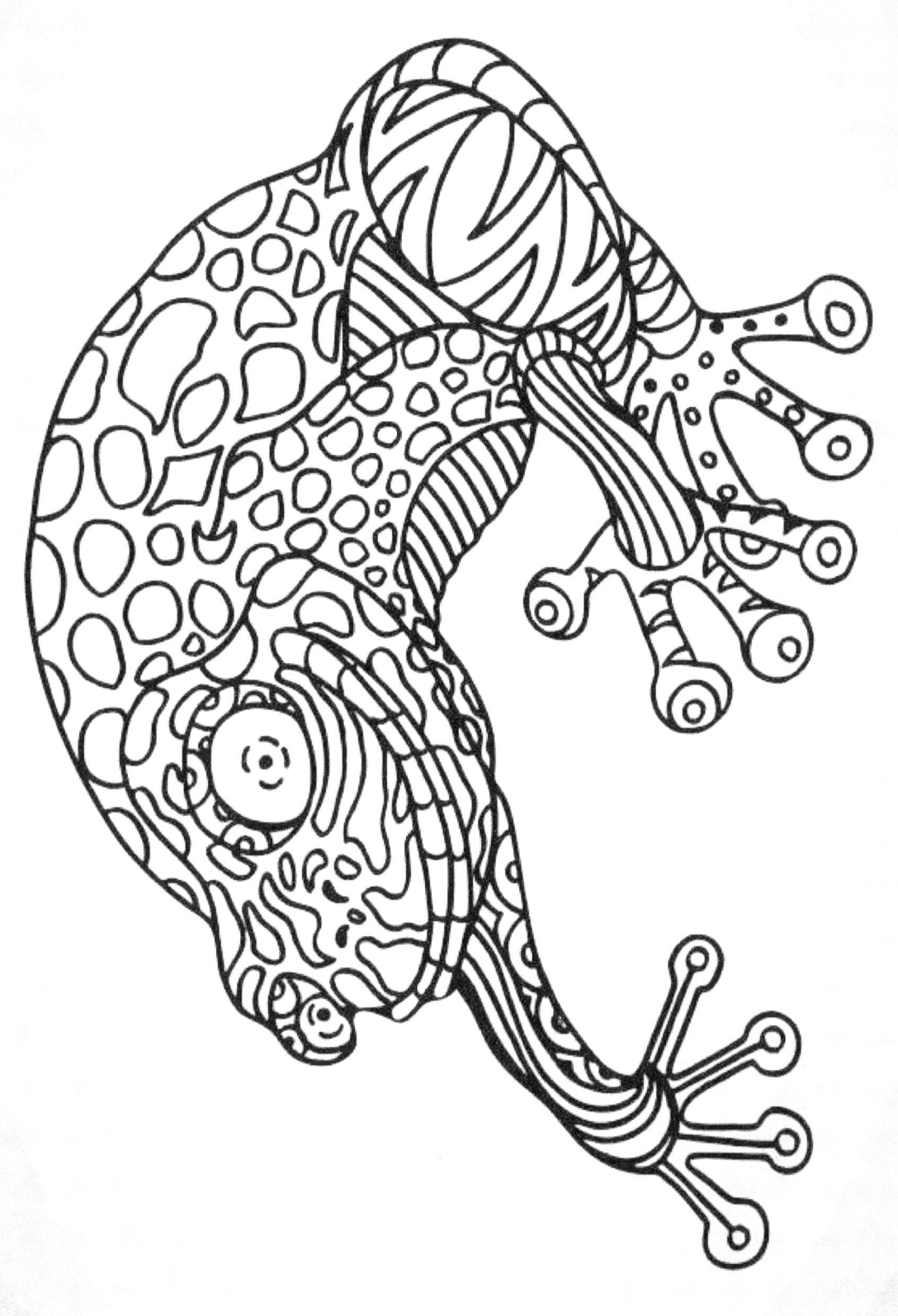

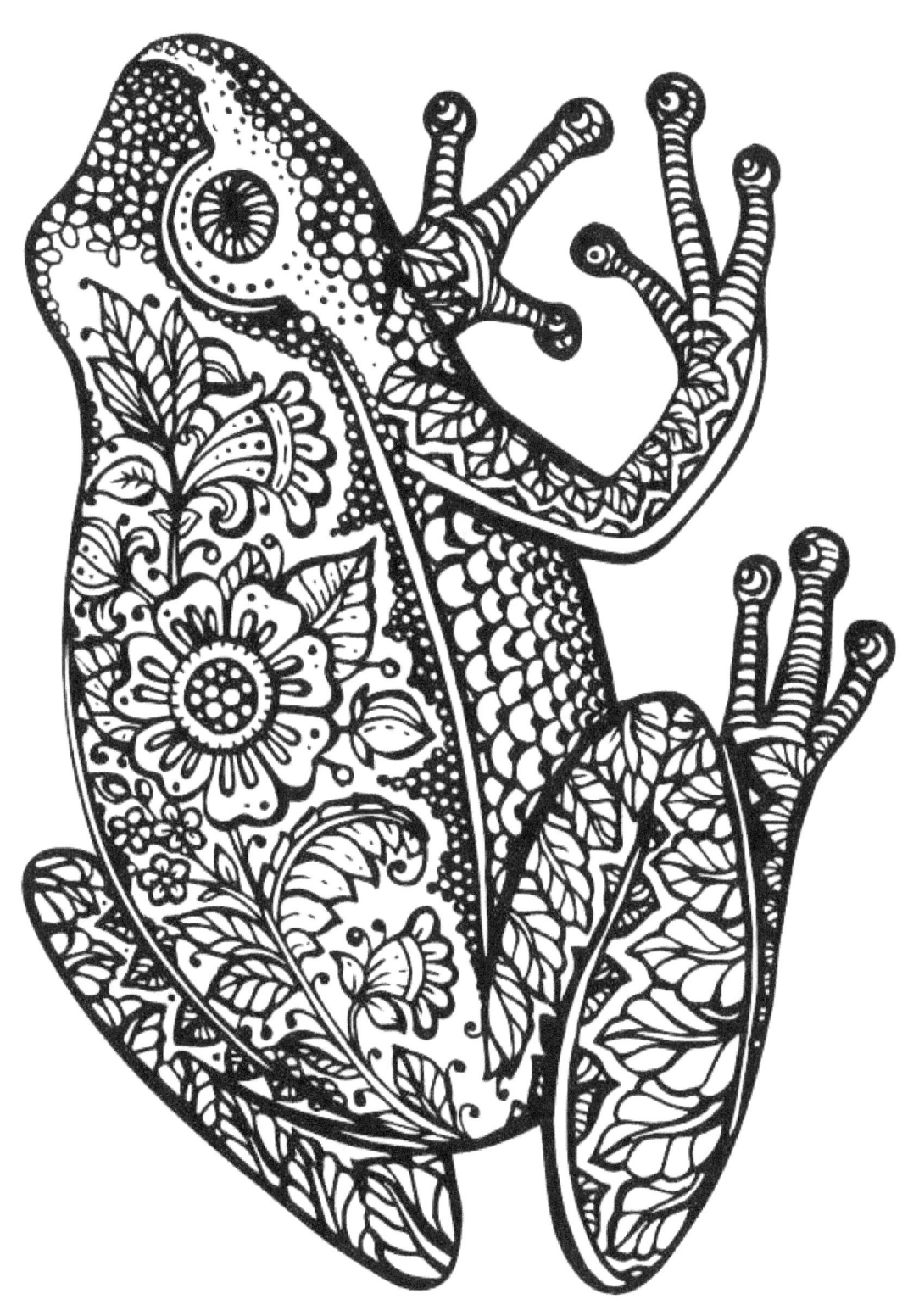

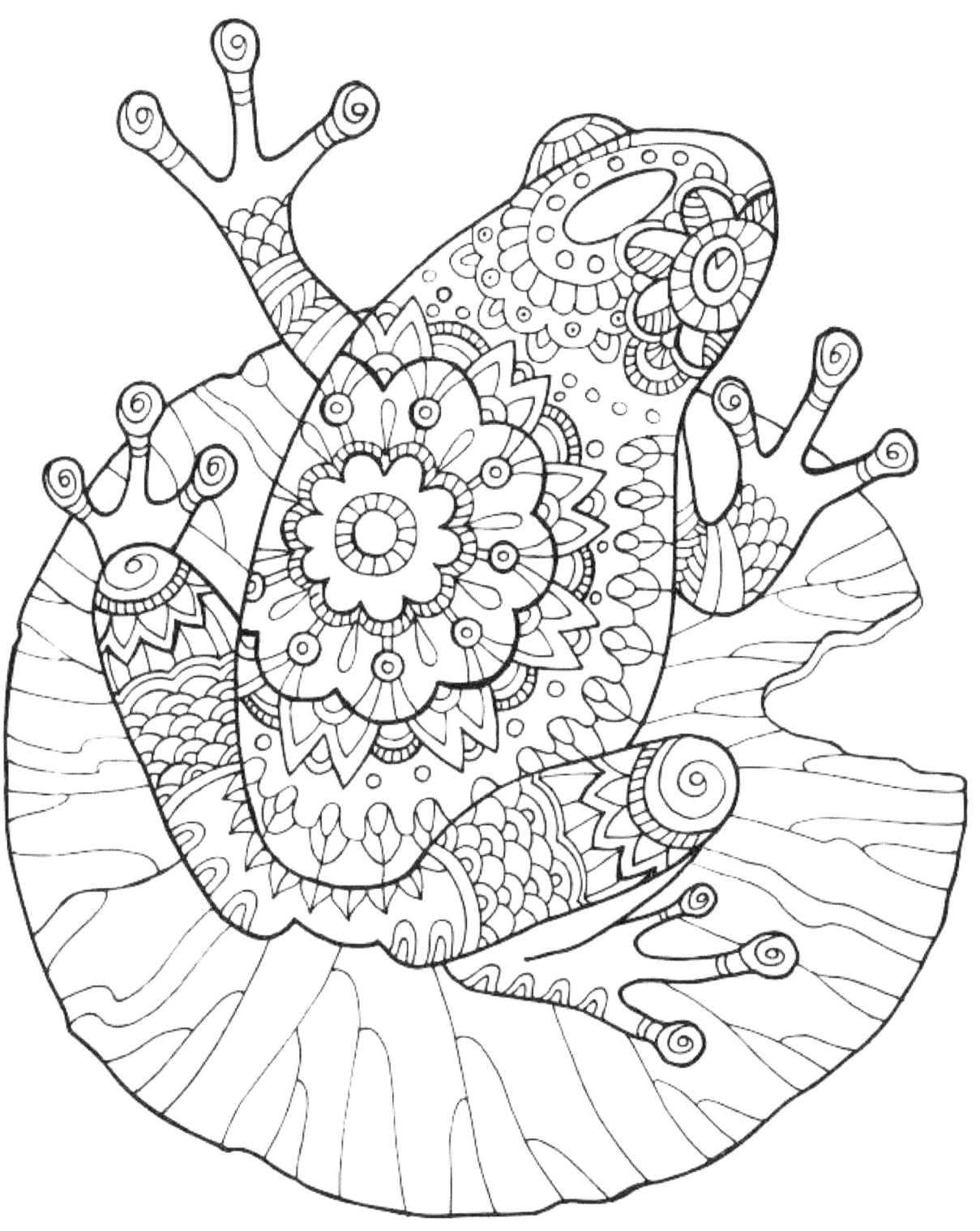

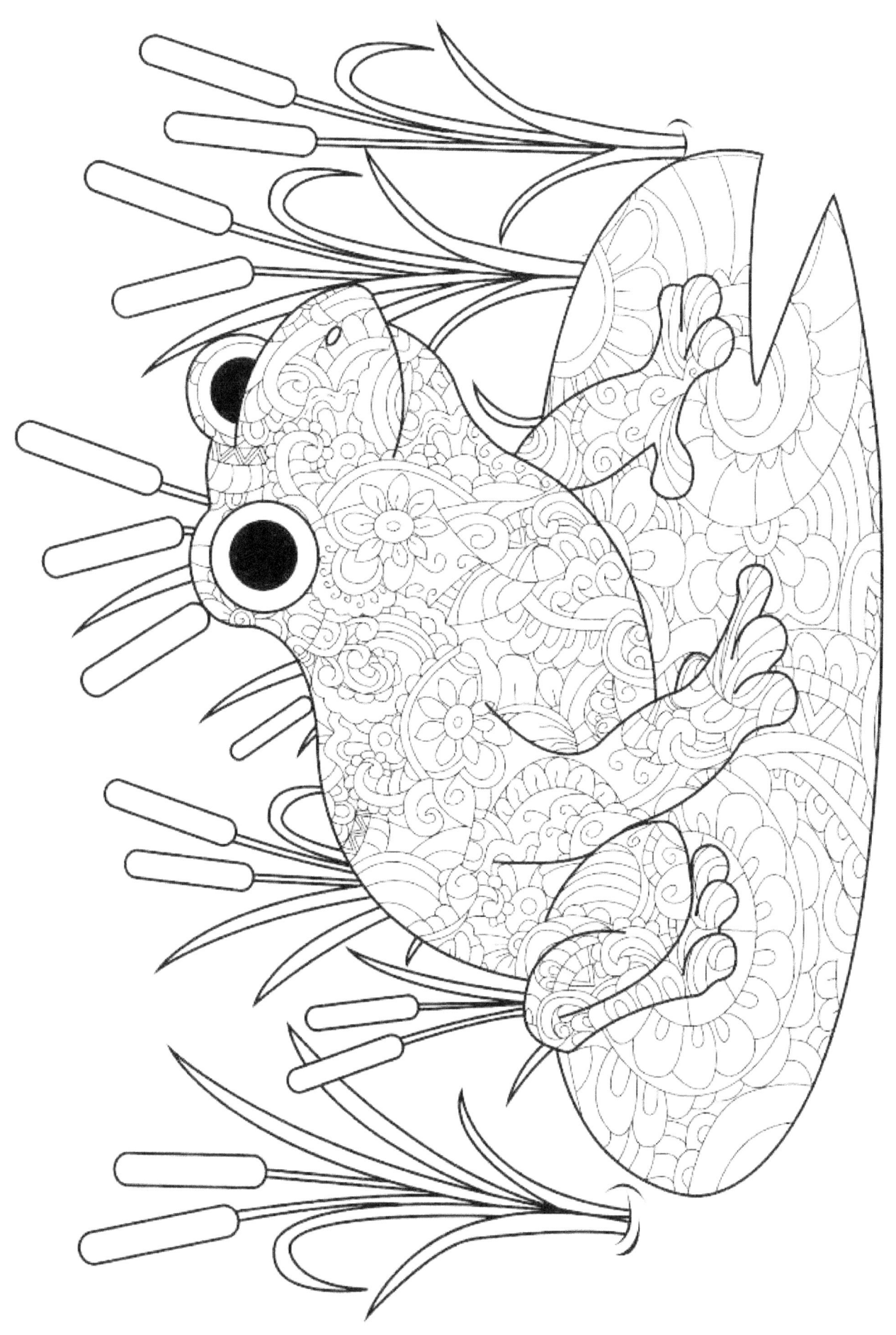

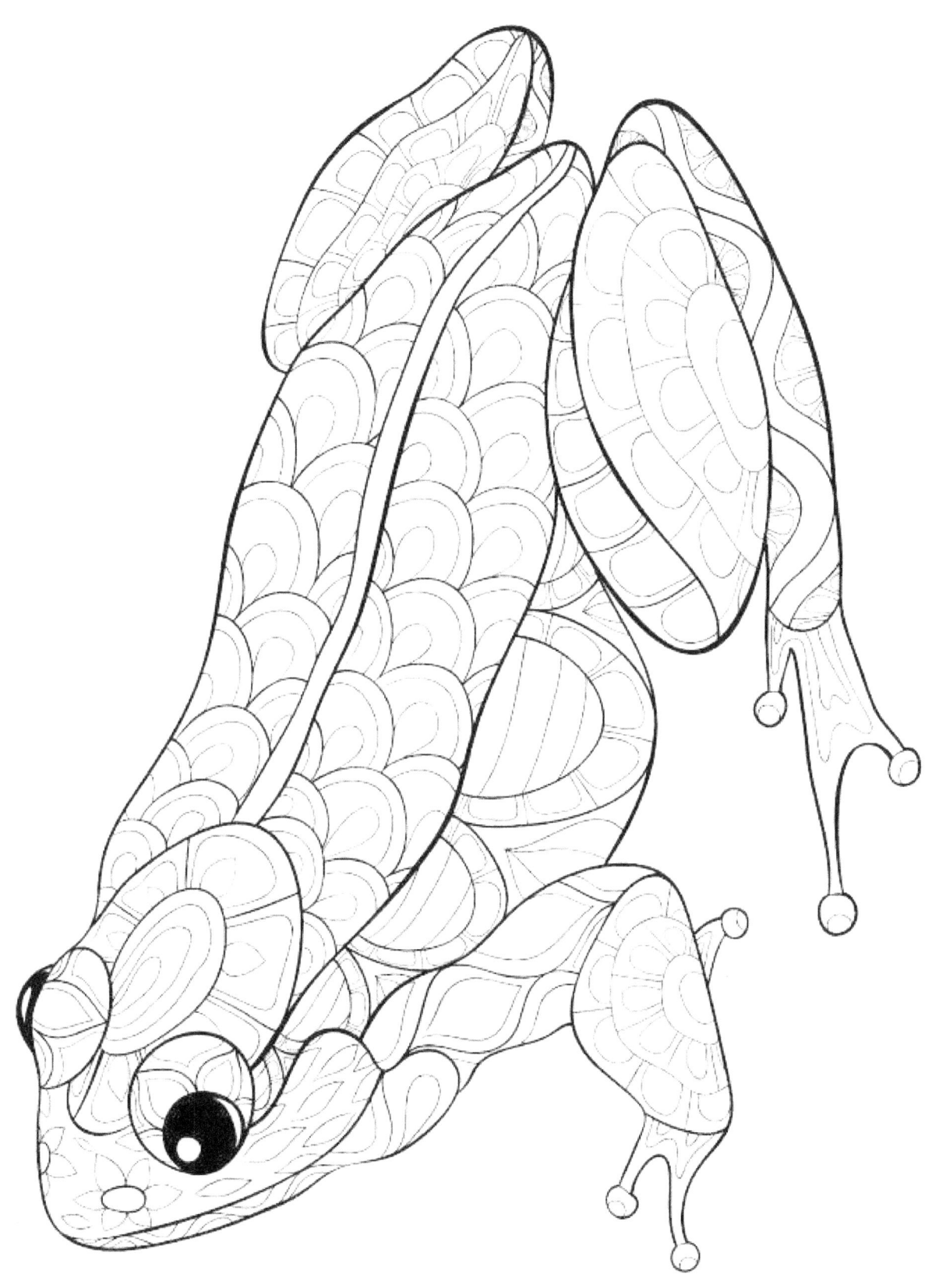

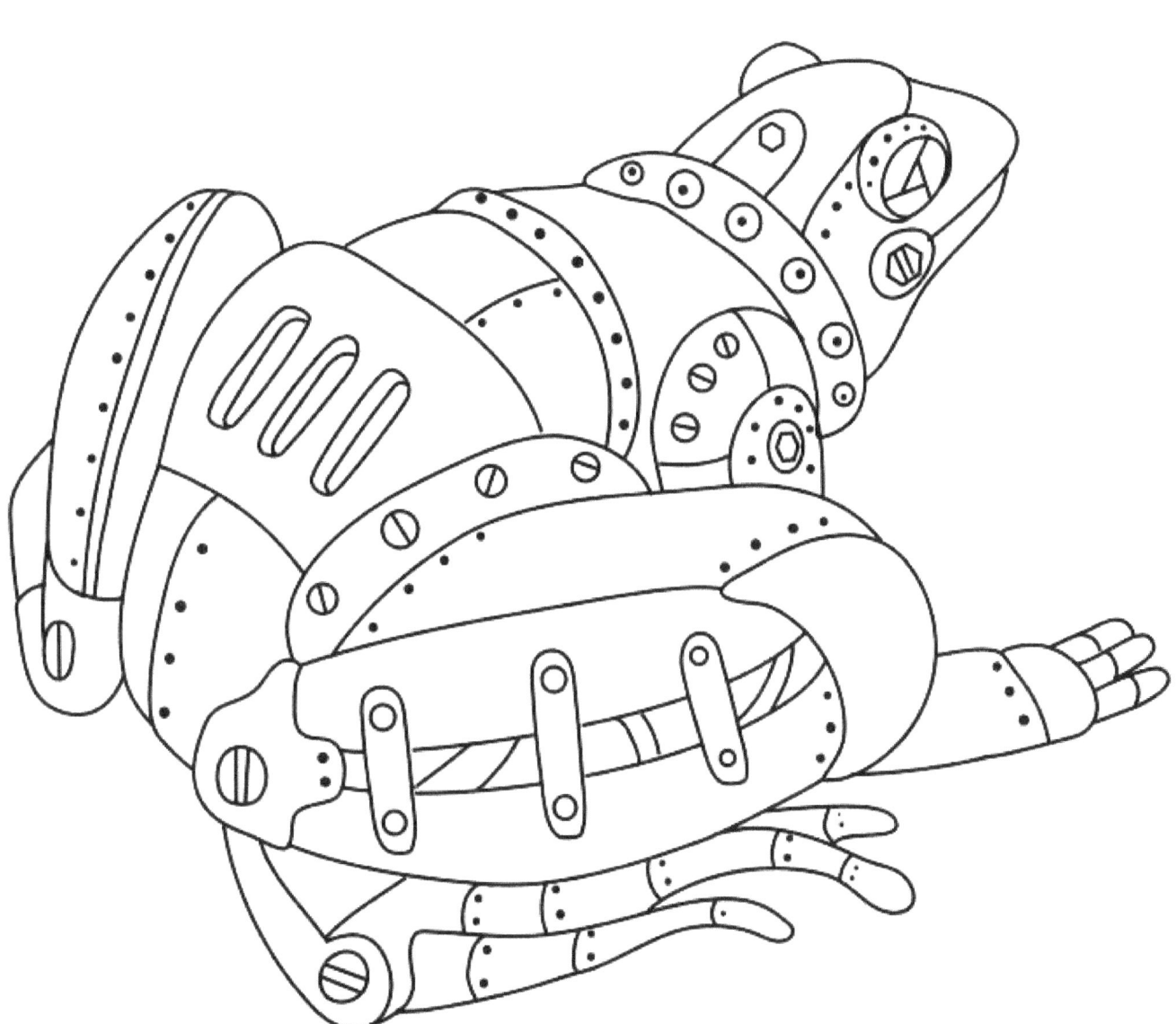

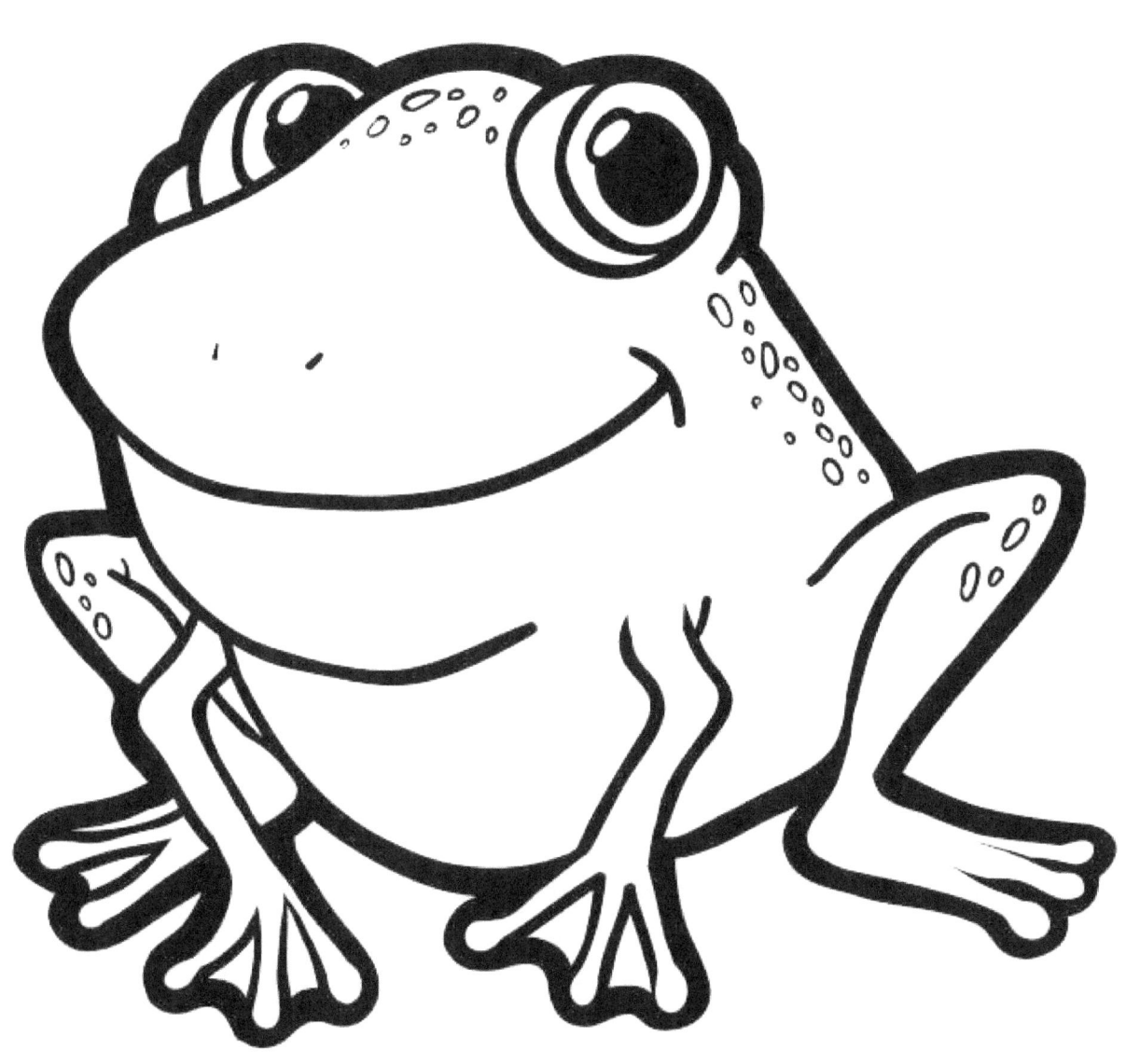

Surprise Bonus Sea Turtles Coloring Pages!

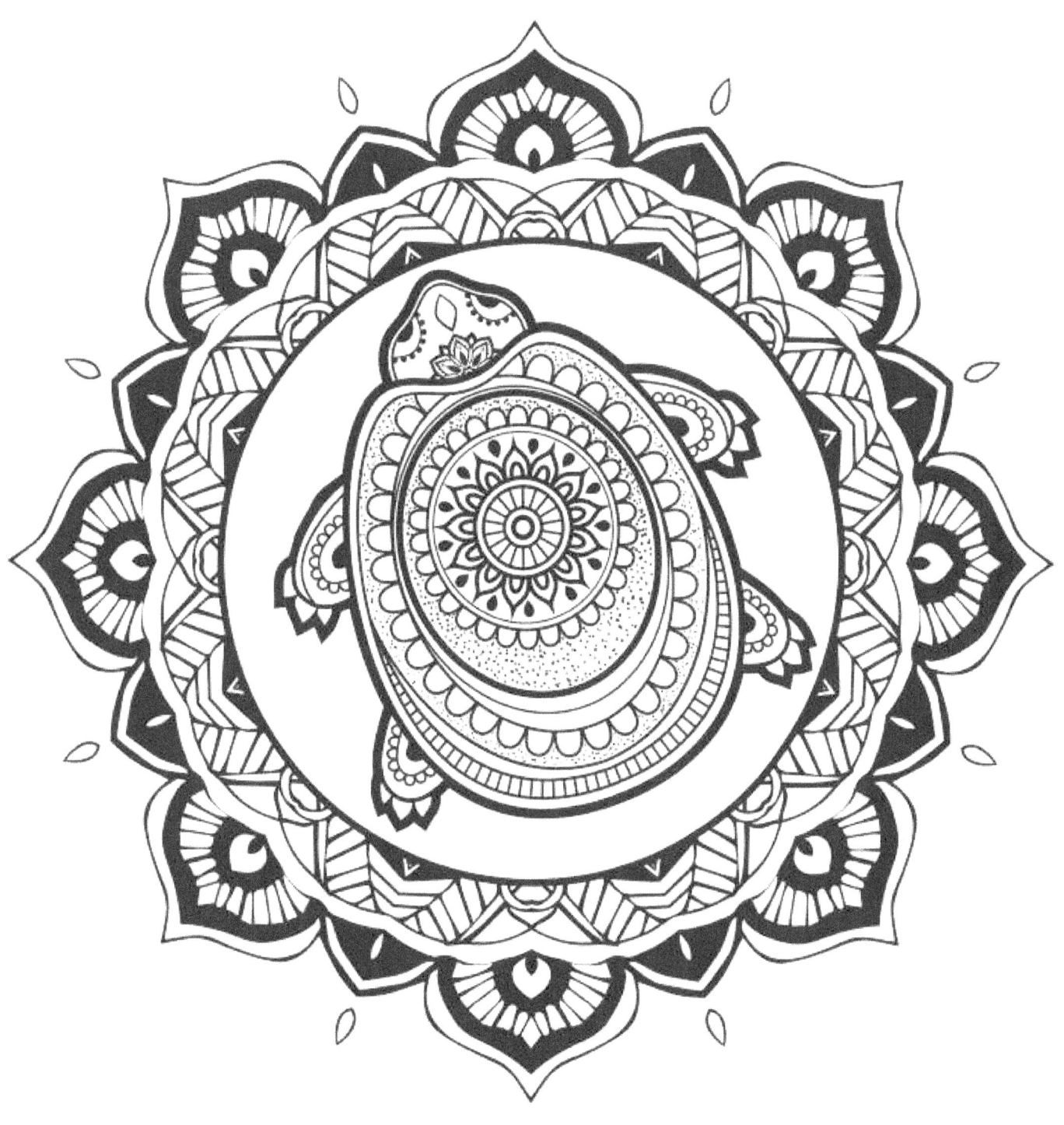

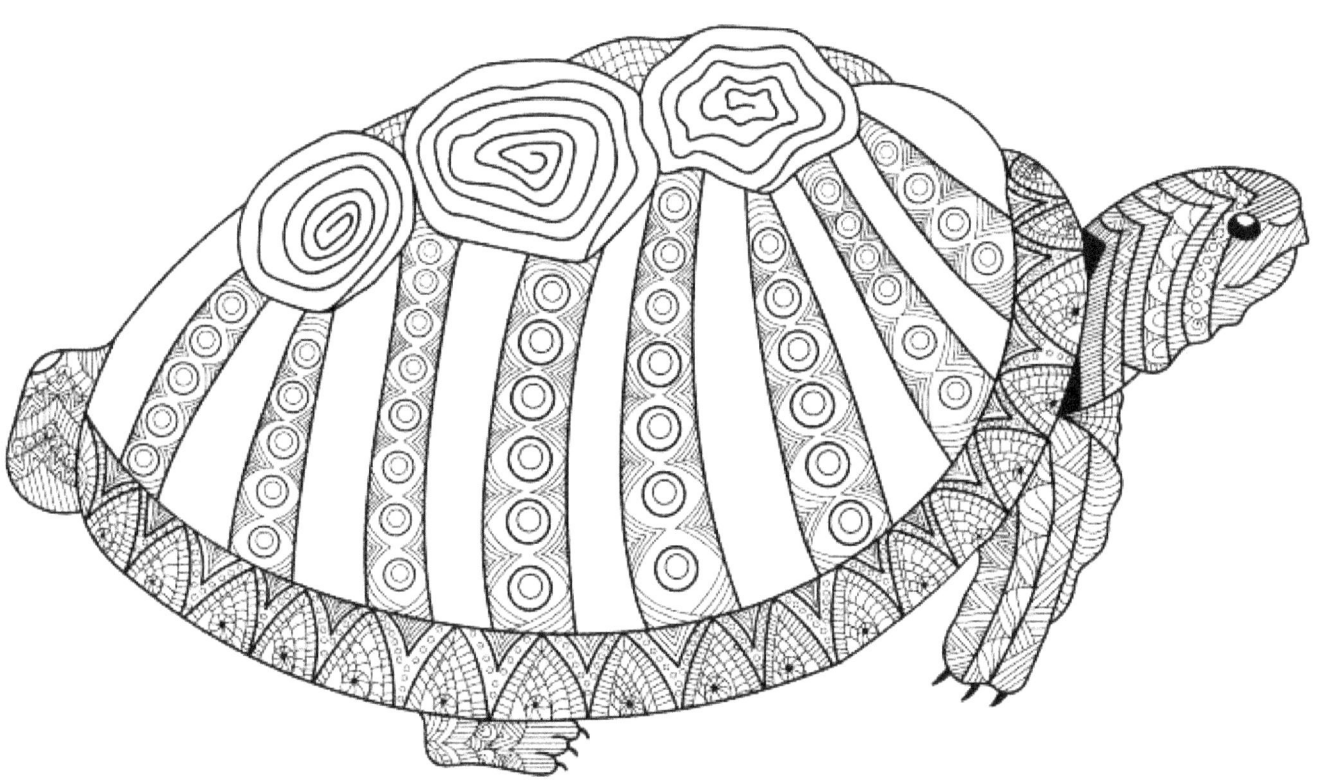

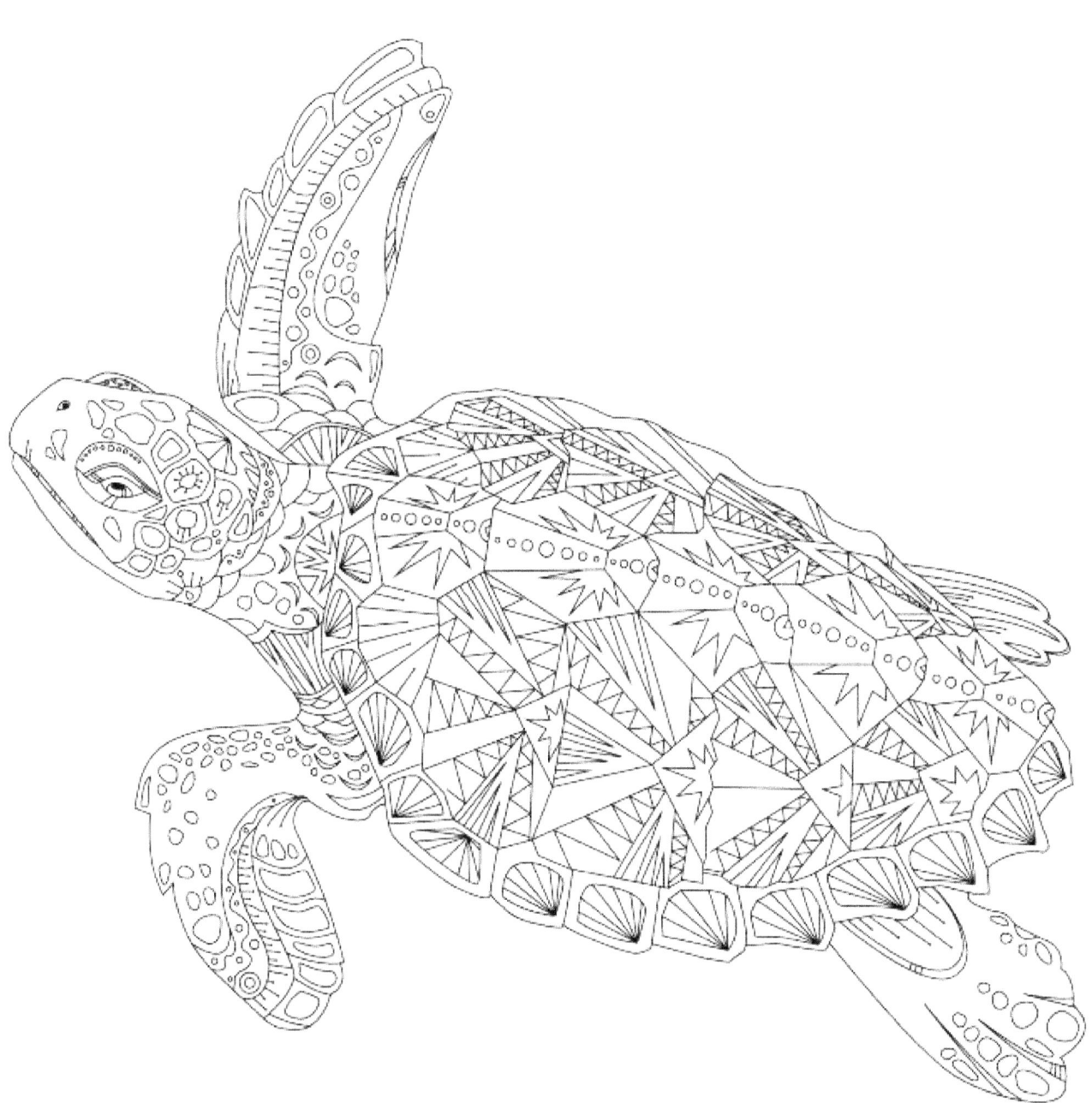

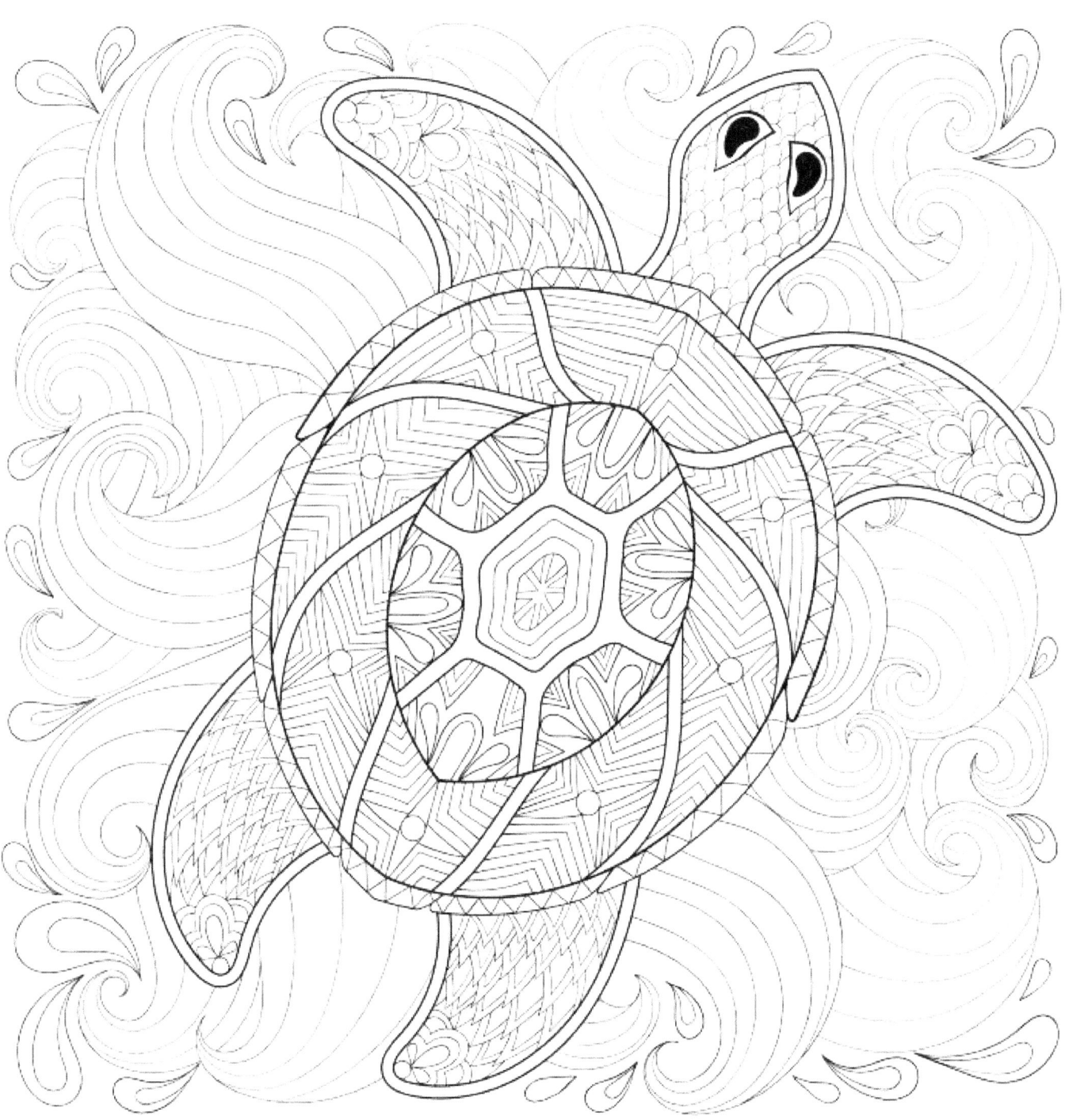

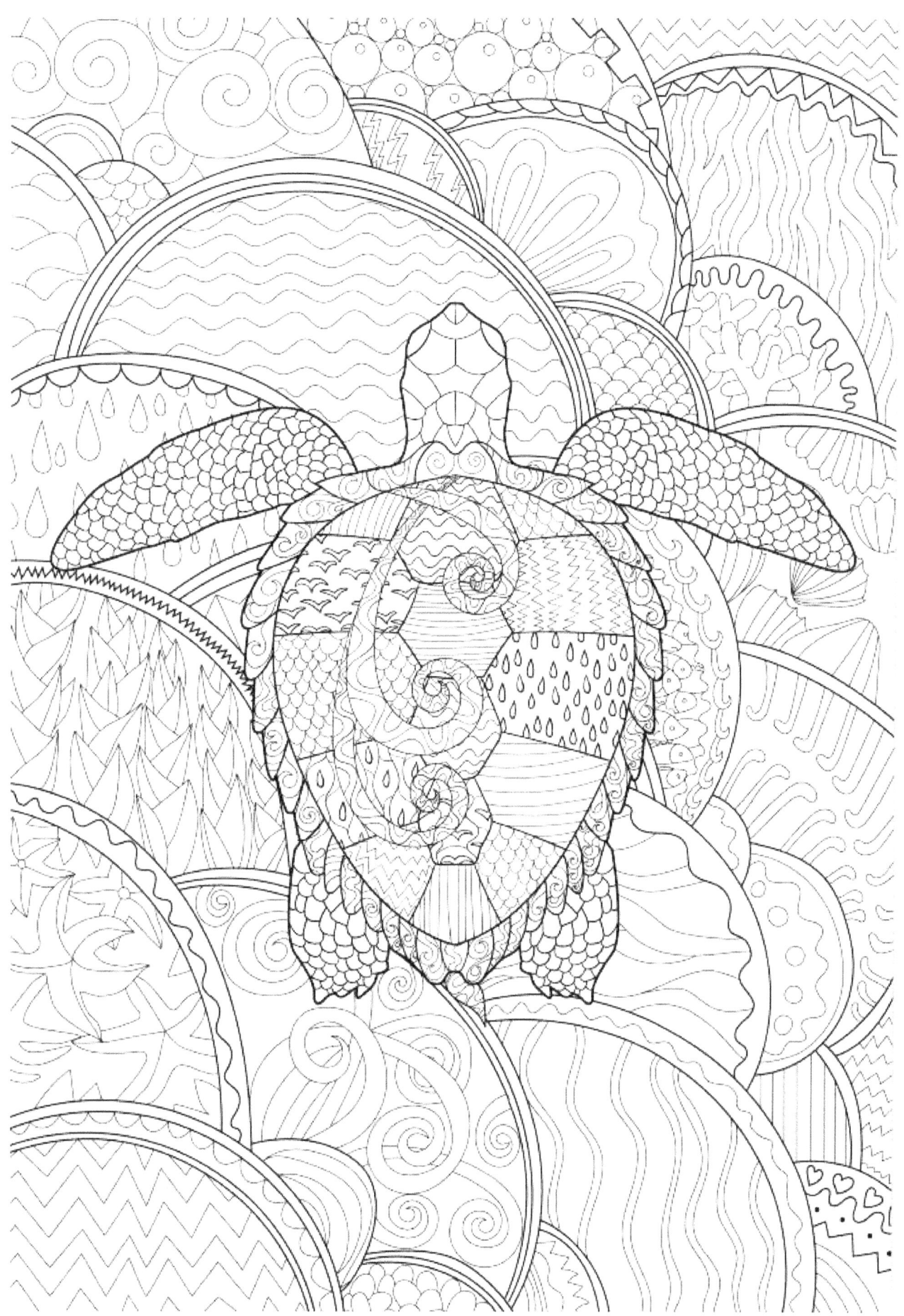

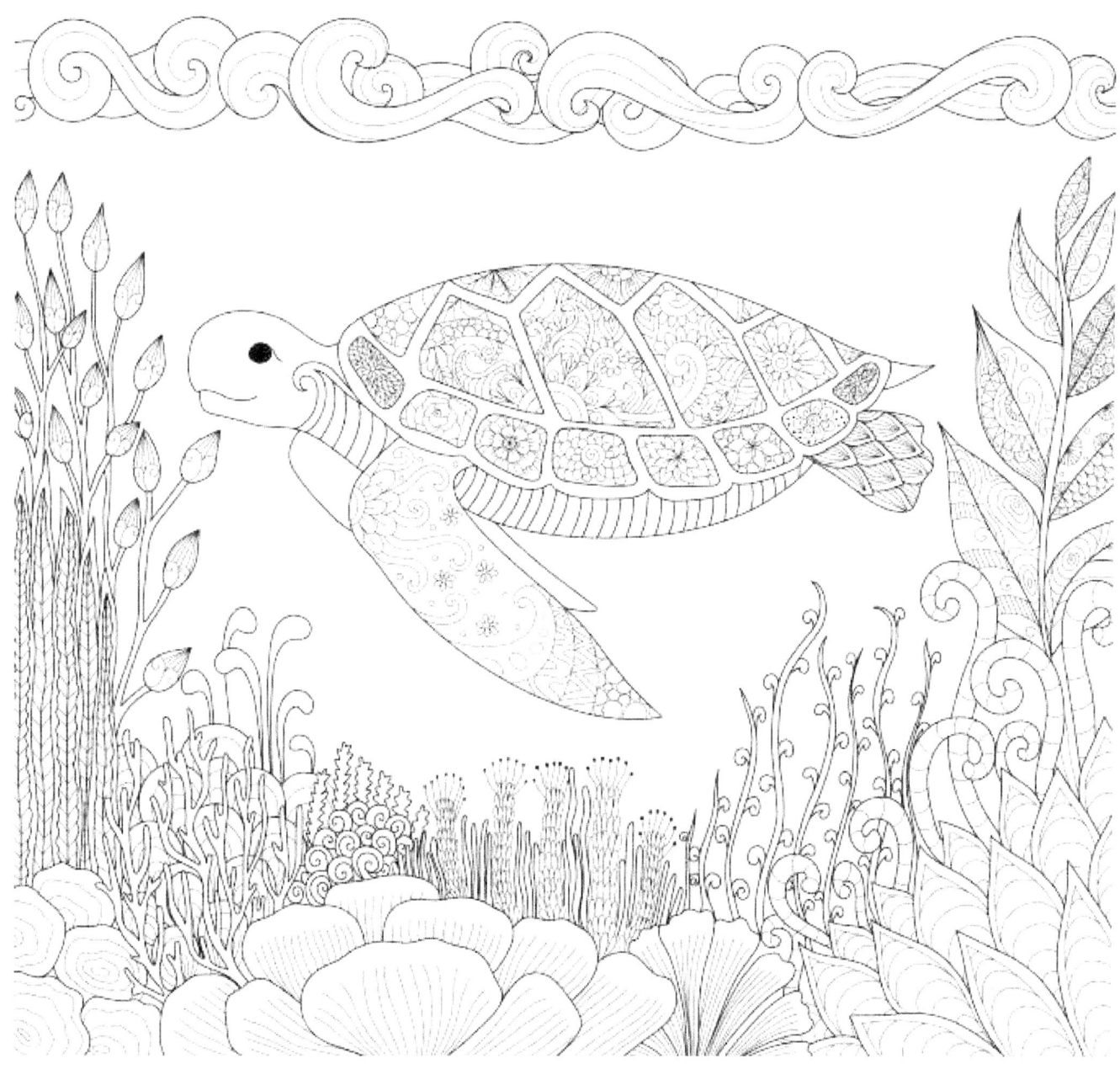

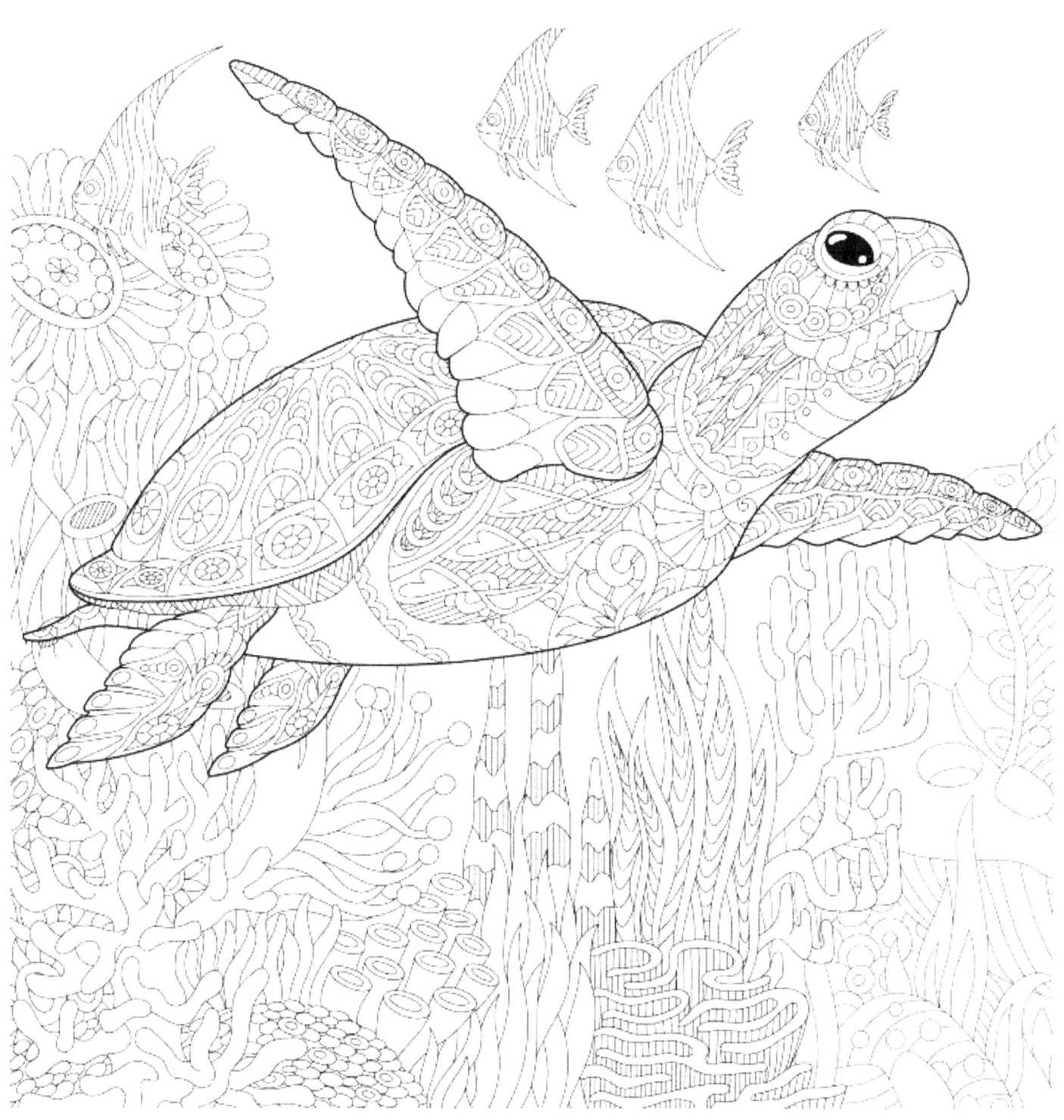

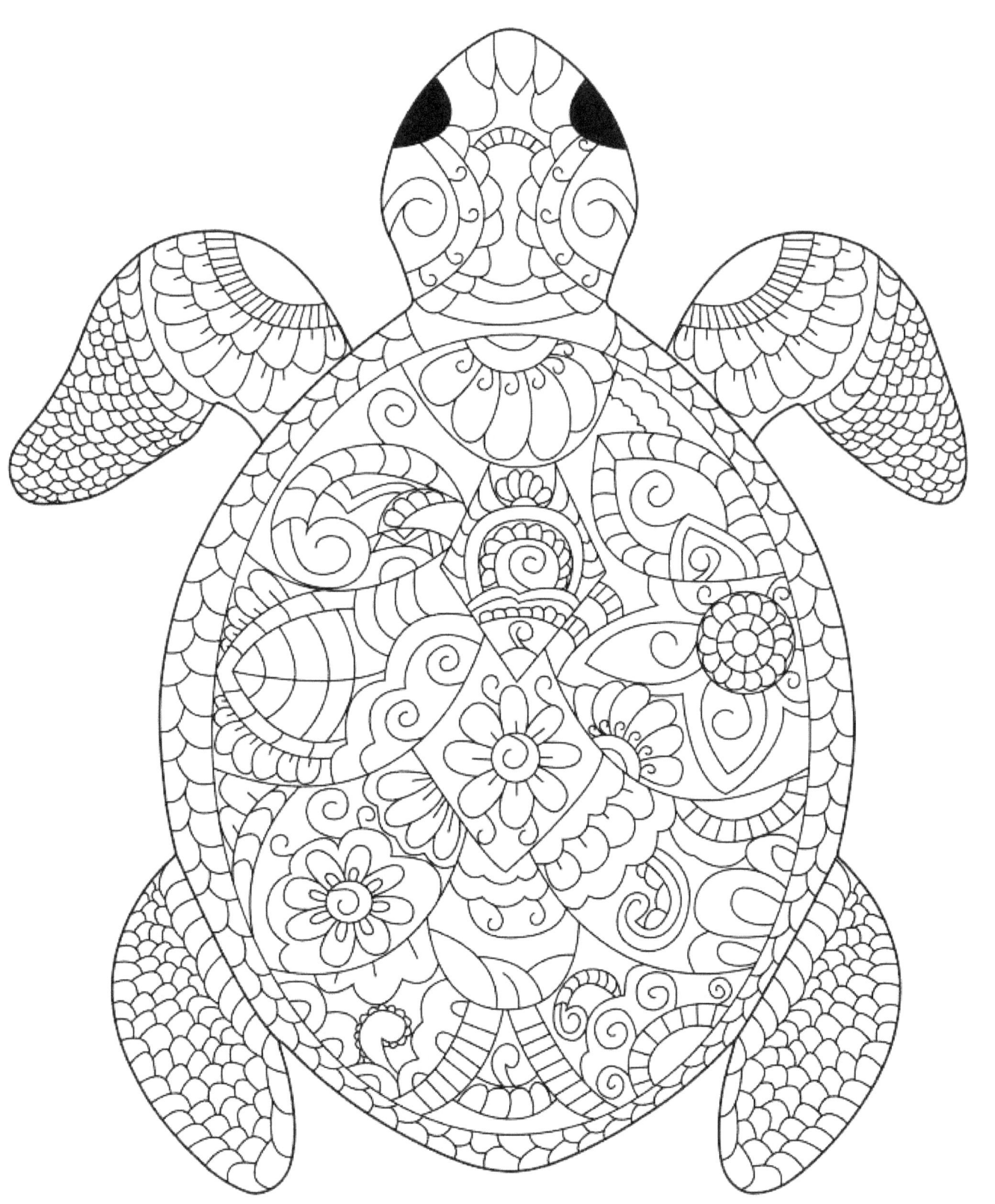

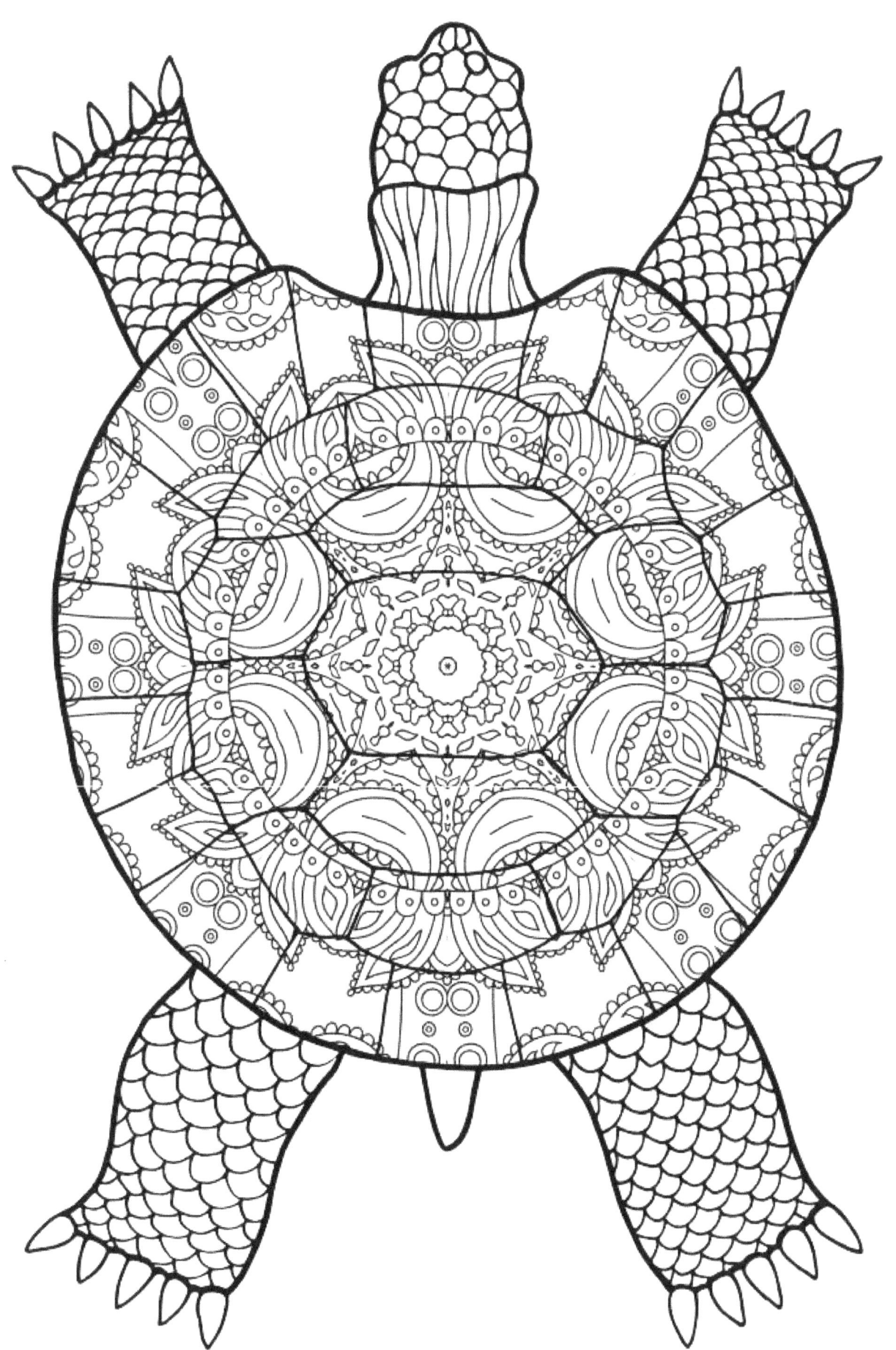

www.ingramcontent.com/pod-product-compliance
Lightning Source LLC
Chambersburg PA
CBHW081300180526
45170CB00007B/2507